YOUR KNOWLEDGE HAS VALUE

- We will publish your bachelor's and master's thesis, essays and papers

- Your own eBook and book - sold worldwide in all relevant shops

- Earn money with each sale

Upload your text at www.GRIN.com and publish for free

Legal Service via Social Media. What could possibly go wrong?

Analysis of the new phenomenon of using of Social Media in Legal Service

Guy Tinsley

Bibliographic information published by the German National Library:

The German National Library lists this publication in the National Bibliography; detailed bibliographic data are available on the Internet at http://dnb.dnb.de.

ISBN: 9783389111437
This book is also available as an ebook.

© GRIN Publishing GmbH
Trappentreustraße 1
80339 München

Print and binding: Books on Demand GmbH, Norderstedt, Germany
Printed on acid-free paper from responsible sources.

The present work has been carefully prepared. Nevertheless, authors and publishers do not incur liability for the correctness of information, notes, links and advice as well as any printing errors.

GRIN web shop: https://www.grin.com/document/1561368

Legal Service via Social Media: What could possibly go wrong?

Background

In November 2017, the author witnessed a Family Court in Nottingham allow a Litigant in Person (LiP) to serve legal notice to his partner (the absent respondent) through the medium of Facebook Messenger. The issues were emotive: The applicant urgently sought disclosure for the whereabouts of their infant children, with whom she had absconded from their home. Evidence presented in Court showed the respondent had a history of substance abuse and mental illness. Consequently, she and their children may have been at risk of physical harm.

While the applicant did not know her physical location, he was able to demonstrate a history of regular, ongoing communication between them via social media. After deliberation, the Judge, at his own instigation, allowed the plaintiff to serve notice, instructing disclosure via Facebook Messenger. He stated his confidence that the respondent would receive and understand the notice and emphasised that the expediency of this method would enable the Court to "move quickly" to next steps, in the event of non-compliance by the respondent.

This report seeks to assess the prevalence of the use of Social Media in Civil Procedure in the UK; its origins, legality and future integration.

Abstract

Social Media: *"forms of electronic communication (such as websites for social networking and microblogging) through which users create online communities to share information, ideas, personal messages, and other content."*[1]

The Civil Procedure Rules

In 1995, a joint enterprise by the National Consumer Council and the BBC's "Law in Action" program published research[2] demonstrating the vast majority of respondents (over 75% on some issues) felt that the Criminal justice System (CJS) was unnecessarily slow, complex and in need of modernisation.

Lord Woolf, commissioned by the Conservative Government to address these issues, called on the CJS to be "just" and "fair", to process cases with "reasonable speed" and be "understandable" to the user; it needed to provide as much "certainty" as cases allowed and be "effective: adequately resourced and organised".[3] In his Final Report of 1996, he also affirmed his strong belief in embracing Information Technology (IT) within the CJS.[4]

Woolf's report contained draft rules of practice, which formed the foundations of The Civil Procedure Act (CPA) 1997 which itself created The Civil Procedure Rules (CPR) 1998 and the Civil Justice Council (CJC), their supervisory body. The CPR, effective from 26 April 1999, govern the service of legal notice in the UK Civil Courts and state their Overriding Objective as "enabling the court to deal with cases justly",[5] reflecting Lord Woolf's recommendations.

---

[1] Merriam-Webster (2016).

[2] Seeking Civil Justice: A Survey of People's Needs and Experiences. The National Consumer Council. 1 Oct 1995.

[3] Ch 1.3 Access to Justice Interim Report by The Right Honourable Justice the Lord Woolf MR, 1995, The National Archive.

[4] Ch 21 Access to Justice Final Report by The Right Honourable the Lord Woolf MR, July 1996, The National Archive.

[5] S.1.1(1) The Civil Procedure Rules 1998.

Woolf's recommendations were developed by the Blair Government through The Courts Act 2003, extending Procedure Rules reforms to the Family and Criminal Courts. Echoing the objectives of CPA 1997,[6] the 2003 Act stated its clear objective to make both the Criminal Procedure Rules[7] and the Family Procedure Rules (FPR)[8] *"accessible, fair and efficient, and…the rules are both simple and simply expressed."*[9] For each, a supervisory body was created – the Criminal Procedure Rules Committee (CPRC) and Family Procedure Rules Committee (FPRC) respectively. The CJC remained unaffected by the 2003 Act.

Since their creation, the CJC, CPRC and FPRC have operated largely independently of each other. They are, however, united in failing to recognise the metamorphosis of IT into "Social Media". Facebook was launched in 2004, and Twitter in 2006, subsequent to the 2003 Act. Yet the use of "Social Media" as a conduit for Legal Service has never been overtly addressed by the CJC, CPRC or FPRC.

Legality

The Criminal Courts are clear about Social Media's use in legal service. Statutes clearly state that a person prosecuted before a Criminal Court must be issued either with an arrest warrant or a summons[10] and this may only be effected by a "Public Prosecutor."[11] It must be by means of a written document[12] and the Criminal Procedure Rules outline how Service of *"every document in a case"* must be served.[13] The only exceptions are where a defendant specifically offers an "electronic address" for service, or where they are given personal, exclusive access to one[14] (i.e. when incarcerated).

While defendants in Criminal cases are naturally averse to any new procedure facilitating their prosecution, the Criminal Courts are also sensitive to Social Media: it is itself becoming a means of committing crime. The Crown Prosecution Service highlights numerous offences capable of being facilitated by Social Media:[15] threats to kill,[16] harassment and stalking,[17] threatening and coercive behaviour[18] (or "Cyberbullying") and breaching reporting restrictions relating to children.[19]

The Criminal Procedure Rules may therefore avoid the use of Social Media by design rather than by accident. Either way, their Rules are certainly the most "simple and simply expressed" regarding how legal service should be effected.

The CPR have had longest to embrace IT's rapid development in social and business communication. Part 6 and Schedule 6A cover the service of documents, but no section explicitly refers to "Social Media" or "Social Media Providers" (SMP's). Without close

---

[6] S.1(3) The Civil Procedure Act 1997.

[7] S.69 (4) (a) and (b), The Courts Act 2003.

[8] S.75 (5) (a) and (b), The Courts Act 2003.

[9] Quoted in both S.69 (4) (a) and (b) and S. 75 (5) (a) and (b), The Courts Act 2003.

[10] S.1(1) Magistrates Court Act 1980.

[11] S.29(5) Criminal Justice Act 2003.

[12] S.29(1) Criminal Justice Act 2003.

[13] S.4 Criminal Procedure Rules 2015.

[14] S 4.6(1) and (2) Criminal Procedure Rules 2015.

[15] "Social Media: Guidelines on prosecuting cases involving communications sent via social media". The Crown Prosecution Service, Code for Crown Prosecutors. www.cps.gov.uk/legal-guidance/social-media-guidelines-prosecuting-cases-involving-communications-sent-social-media. Accessed 13/08/2018.

[16] S.16 Offences Against The Person Act 1861.

[17] S.2, 2A, 4 / 4A, Protection from Harassment Act 1997.

[18] S.76, Serious Crime Act 2015.

[19] S.49 of the Children and Young Persons Act 1933 and S.45 of the Youth Justice and Criminal Evidence Act 1999.

scrutiny, the opportunity to embrace Social Media is easily missed. Section 6.3 covers other, older methods of service – first class post, personal service or document exchange (DX), but they require a respondent to occupy a physical address at which notice can be served. Section 6.3(1)(d) discusses "other means of electronic communication", with referral to schedule 6A, where such service is only permitted specifically with the respondent's prior consent for each proposed method of electronic communication.

It is only at S.6.3(1)(e) that "*any method authorised by the court under rule 6.15*" is authorised. At S.6.15, finally, "*Service of the claim form by an alternative method or at an alternative place*" is permitted, where it "*appears to the court there is a good reason*" to so allow.

Confusingly, while 6.15 does not refer to Schedule 6A, sections 9.1, 9.2 and 9.3 of Schedule 6A expressly refer to 6.15, detailing requirements to formally apply for "alternative" service under 6.15, covering requisite evidence, the reason the application is sought, the proposed alternative method or place of delivery and why the applicant considers this method more appropriate than the standard means. Section 9.2 replicates these requirements in the event that such an application has already been made, but also requires a statement of the likelihood of the respondent to receive the documents. S.9.3 gives examples of elements of such an application in respect of an alternative postal address,[20] voicemail or SMS[21] and e-mail[22] and all sections demonstrate a clear statement of the need for reliability of the method in reaching the respondent. But nowhere is "Social Media" expressly even mentioned.

Despite this omission, it appears that Section 6.15, supported by S.9.3 of Schedule 6A allows service of legal notices by "*an alternative method or at an alternative place*", which, with the court's approval and following a successful application may be effected via Social Media. This is certainly a narrow legal aperture for the applicant, and difficult to spot by the layman, often nowadays a LiP (below). But once through it, subsequent boundaries are highly elastic: There are no examples of the "good reason" the court requires to authorise such service. It may just deem it so.

Landmarks

A "landmark case" would normally rescue the law from uncertainty: *Entores v Miles*[23] identified how the new "Telex" machine separated instantaneous communications from the *Adams v Lindsell*[24] "Postal Rule". It recognised that communication systems had advanced exponentially and the rules needed to advance with them. Since then, however the phrase "instantaneous communications" has also been lost in statute. What is Social Media, if not instantaneous communication?

In *Blaney v Persons Unknown (October 2009)*[25] the applicant, a political "blogger", sought an injunction against an anonymous individual impersonating him on Twitter, to cease his posts (along with further actions and disclosure) as they allegedly breached the applicant's Intellectual Property Rights (IPR).

Due to the Defendant's anonymity in "cyberspace" and apparent reliance thereon, the High Court permitted that the injunction be served via Twitter under CPR 6.15. The message sent to the Defendant's Twitter account included a link to the injunction, which the Defendant would have received as soon as he logged into his account. The court was therefore satisfied that Twitter was both an effective and reliable method of service.

---

[20] Section 9.3(1), Schedule 6A, The Civil Procedure Rules.

[21] Section 9.3(2) Schedule 6A, The Civil Procedure Rules.

[22] Section 9.3(3), Schedule 6A, The Civil Procedure Rules.

[23] Entores v Miles Far East Corp [1955] 2 QB 327.

[24] Adams v Lindsell (1818) 1B & Ald. 681.

[25] Blaney v Persons Unknown [2009] (unreported).

It is a notable quirk that Twitter itself was an integral factor of the case and the medium through which the alleged breach had taken place: it was the location the defendant occupied to commit his breach. The question of Twitter's appropriateness for alternative service, had Twitter never been involved, was never addressed.

The applicant's alternative would have been to pursue a *Norwich Pharmacal Order* (NPO)[26] against Twitter. This comparatively lengthy and costly legal process allows an order for disclosure to be granted against an innocent third party. Originally used for cases involving IPR, NPO's have also been applied in cases of fraud,[27] breach of contract,[28] breach of confidence,[29] breach of privacy under the Data Protection Act 1989[30] and defamation by publication of information online.[31] By 2009,[32] NPO's had become a contentious issue, with some Judges seeing them as a "last resort"[33] and others seeing them as both flexible and useful.[34]

Despite the *"Blaney's Blarney Order"* presenting a quick, simple and cost-free alternative, it did not "open the floodgates": it is unreported. Ironically, despite relying on a "public" channel, it is believed Blaney (himself a lawyer) prefers the matter to remain private.

In March 2011, The Daily Telegraph[35] reported that Hastings County Court ordered a debtor to be served legal documents via Facebook. The solicitor, Hilary Thorpe persuasively cited an Australian Supreme Court case from 2008[36] involving similar problems in contacting and bringing a debtor to court. The same year, the Australian courts had also rejected such an application,[37] overtly citing concerns about the ease of creating false identities and difficulty of validating the creators of Facebook pages. Ms Thorpe avoided this reference, though!

AKO Capital[38] was also overlooked. It preceded the Hastings case by a month and is now the "landmark case" for service via Social Media: For the first time the High Court allowed legal service through Facebook's Messenger service, whose use had grown rapidly since its expansion to iOS and Android devices in August 2010. Notably, it stressed that the relevant Facebook account must belong to the person in question and that the intended recipient checked the account regularly and often. But *AKO Capital* and *Blaney* were absent in Hastings: Woolf's desire to embrace IT in the courts was not reflected in information exchanges between them!

---

[26] Norwich Pharmacal Co. & Others v Customs and Excise Commissioners [1974] AC 133.

[27] Kensington International Ltd v (1) Republic of Congo & (2) Vitol Services Ltd 4 [2007] EWCA Civ. 1128).

[28] Ashworth Hospital Authority v MGN Ltd [2002] UKHL 29.

[29] (British Steel Corporation v Granada Television Ltd HL [1981] 1 All ER 435 .

[30] (Nikitin v Richards Butler LLP and others [2007] EWHC 173 (QB), Hughes v Carratu International plc [2006] EWHC 1791 (QB).

[31] Smith v ADVFN Ltd & Ors (No2) Reference [2008] EWHC 1797 (QB); *Totalise PLC v The Motley Fool Ltd* & another. [2001] E.M.L.R. 29.

[32] Professional Liability Claims: Norwich Pharmacal Proceedings and Human Rights. A presentation to the Professional Negligence Lawyers' Association on 25.06.09 by JONATHAN BELLAMY, 39 Essex Street, London WC2R 3AT.

[33] Lightman J, Mitsui & Co Ltd v Nexen Petroleum UK Ltd**. [2005] EWHC 625 (Ch)**; Langley J in Nikitin 2007 (citation above).

[34] The Queen (on the application of Binyan Mohamed) v Secretary of State for Foreign & Commonwealth Affairs (No.2) [2010] EWCA Civ 158; Thomas LJ and Lloyd-Jones LJ.

[35] "British lawyer uses Facebook to serve court summons". The Daily Telegraph, 14 March 2011.

[36] *MKM Capital Pty Ltd v Corbo* & Poyser ACT Sup Ct, (No SC 608 of 2008).

[37] Citigroup Property Limited v Wekaroon [2008] QDC 174 (Queensland District Court – 16 April 2008.

[38] AKO Capital LLC and Master Fund Limited v TFS Derivatives & Others UKHC [17 February 2012].

Progress

"Substituted service" via Social Media[39] is progressive and global. Along with Australia, New Zealand saw Facebook used for legal service in 2008[40] and Canada in 2009.[41] The UK is an "early adopter" nevertheless: Ireland[42] and South Africa[43] set their precedents in 2012.

But the USA, home of Facebook and Twitter, refused such an application in 2012. The Court asserted *"anyone can make a Facebook profile using real, fake or incomplete information"*.[44] Only in March 2015 was an applicant permitted to serve divorce papers through a Facebook account;[45] the USA has allowed such permissions only sparingly since.

By 2014, this "substituted service" was established in the UK. *Re A Debtor*[46] saw District Judge Lethem order summons, again of an elusive bankrupt, for examination under the Insolvency Act 1986. In 2015, *The Bussey Law Firm PC*[47] affirmed concerns raised in Australia, the US and *AKO Capital*, highlighting the complex issues of proving user identities, password and account security and the likelihood of "hackers" creating "fake" profiles. Aware of these risks, the CPR nevertheless qualify substituted service through social media, as an "alternative method", where the court deems "good reason" to do so. Despite its potential to do so, it has not spread rapidly through the Civil Courts. Many lawyers, and perhaps courts, remain unaware of the facility. But it still spread to the Family Courts.

The Family

In February 2017, in *RE T (a child)*,[48] Holman HHJ addressed the use of Facebook to locate a birth parent required to consent to an adoption:[49]

"….I do not for one moment suggest that Facebook should be the first method used, but it does seem to be a useful tool in the armoury... Of course, not everyone is on Facebook but, in this particular case, a relatively socially disadvantaged young mother in [X] has been found very rapidly by that means."

Rather than allowing alternative service, Holman HHJ instead discussed the ability to dispense with service, specifically identifying S.6.36 of the FPR, but not before emphasising the "mandatory" requirement for Courts to provide "adequate service" to both natural parents in an adoption case.[50] The FPR have added complexities: they are divided first by differentiation between Matrimonial and Civil Partnership orders[51] and

---

[39] Court "likes" Notification via Social Media, March 2, 2015, Stephen Leslie, https://blogs.lexisnexis.co.uk/randi/court-likes-notification-via-social-media.

[40] *Axe Market Gardens v Craig Axe* CIV: 2008-485-2676 (New Zealand High Court).

[41] *Knott* Estate *v. Sutherland*, [2009] A.J. No. 1539 (Alta. Q.B.), Canada.

[42] Daly v Lynch [2012], Ireland.

[43] CMC Woodworking Machinery (Property) Ltd. v Pieter Odendaal Kitchens (Unreported case no. 6846/2006, 03 August 2012).

[44] Fortunato v Chase Bank USA n.a. 11 Civ.6608 (JFK) 2012.

[45] *Baidoo v. Blood-Dzraku* (2015 NY Slip Op 25096).

[46] Re A Debtor (No 0274 of 2010), County Court of Tunbridge Wells.

[47] The Bussey Law Firm PC, Timothy Raymond Bussey v Jason Page (aka Jay Page) [2015] EWHC 563 (QB).

[48] Re T (a child) [2017] EWFC 19.

[49] Re T (a child) [2017] EWFC 19, (at 21).

[50] Re T (a Child) [2017] EWFC 19, (at 9 & 13).

[51] The Family Procedure Rules 2010, 6.3 – 6.22.

then orders outside of that description, notably involving children and other vulnerable people,[52] applying a potential myriad of special considerations.

For legal service via Social Media, the FPR, updated in 2010, are interpreted in a process similar to the CPR of 1997. For the first category, S.6.19 allows service by an *"alternative method or at an alternative place"* where it deems "good reason" to so, with virtually identical criteria to S.6.15 CPR.

For the second category, involving children and other vulnerable parties, it is S.35 which appears to cover service by an *"alternative method or at an alternative place."* However, it cites S.6.19, with the addendum that it: *"applies to any document in proceedings as it applies to an application for a matrimonial or civil partnership order and reference to the respondent in that rule is modified accordingly".* This is another narrow, obscure legal aperture. If these few words are sufficient to allow Social Media to convey service affecting children are they "understandable" (per Woolf) or, under the Courts Act, "simple and simply expressed"?

Holman HHJ avoided both 6.19 and 6.35 of the FPR in *Re T (a child)*: the use of Facebook for delivery of service represented dispensation of service altogether (per S.6.36, above) rather than an alternative method. Accepting that expediting service through Facebook would benefit the child[53], Holman HHJ opined that the expediency may adversely affect the mother, who needed time to consider the situation before service was delivered[54]. His solution was to abandon the hearing, concluding that it allowed *"sufficient time for proper service upon the mother."* By inference, he did not consider using Facebook as "proper service".

The hearing, albeit short, addressed the rights of applicants, respondents and children. It explored the efficiency of Facebook in locating an absent party and its potential role as means of substituted service. It suggested that once an applicant is located, Family Courts should revert to more "traditional" methods of legal service. It also identified the onus on the authorities to locate respondents, rather than parties. Most notably, however, it avoided allowing service via Social Media.

Re T (a child) also broached the criteria where a Family Court may find requisite "good reason" to allow service via Social Media. The FPR match the CPR's scope. But a rationale that permission from one court constitutes permission in another is illogical: The Courts Act 2003 identifies them as wholly separate entities, with bespoke supervising bodies and differently drafted Procedure Rules. Again, the elasticity of legal boundaries once the paths to "alternative methods" and "good reason" have been navigated appear to be looser still.

Regulation

The Law has certainly not by-passed SMP's. The new EU-wide GDPR[55] strictly regulates what Internet Service Providers (ISP's) can do with an individual's personal information. Article 4 defines "personal data" *as*

"any information relating to an identified or identifiable and natural person (data subject)" and that

"processing means any operation...performed on personal data" and includes *"disclosure by transmission, dissemination or otherwise making available."*[56]

---

[52] The Family Procedure Rules 2010, 6.23 – 6.39.

[53] At 26, Section 1(3) of the Adoption and Children Act 2002.

[54] Re T (a Child) [2017] EWFC 19 (22-27 inclusive).

[55] Regulation (EU) 2016/679 of the European Parliament and of the Council of 27 April 2016 on the protection of natural persons with regard to the processing of personal data and on the free movement of such data, and repealing Directive 95/46/EC (General Data Protection Regulation).

[56] Article 4, GDPR. "Definitions" (1) and (2).

It places clear responsibility on an ISP for the processing of personal data.[57] Where such processing[58] may lead to a "natural person" suffering: *"discrimination...damage to the reputation...other significant economic or social disadvantage"*

and goes on to expressly safeguard personal data processing of vulnerable natural persons, particularly children.

The GDPR offers some exemptions[59] to "Controllers"[60] and "Processors",[61] (applicable to ISP's and SMP's), stating that they;

"should be exempt from liability if it proves that it is not in any way responsible for the damage." But it goes on to rule that where breaches have occurred,

"data subjects should receive full and effective compensation for the damage they have suffered".

The GDPR refer expressly "without prejudice" to the provisions of EU Directive 2000/31/EC, which also offers exemption of liability to a service provider where they are a "mere conduit" of a communication and do not *"modify"* or *"alter the integrity"* of the information transmitted.[62] Despite these references the GDPR appear to place a greater onus of proof of innocence on ISP's and SMP's, requiring them to establish that they are not *"in any way responsible for the damage"*; effectively, the service provider must decide whether any transmission is genuinely actionable or not – itself a complex and involved exercise! The Data Protection Act 2018,[63] UK legislation effected to clarify the GDPR, supports these assertions, with its only deviations allowing access by law enforcement and counter-terrorism agencies to otherwise private electronic communications.

"A Safe Haven For Terrorists"

The UK's sensitivity to these rights of access and cooperation between law enforcement agencies and SMP's was highlighted in the inquest following the murder of Fusilier Lee Rigby[64]. Following this tragedy, a Government-appointed Committee analysed the responsibility of SMP's for the content of transmissions passing through them. Facebook[65] effectively summed up a universal approach among SMP's:[66]

"they enable users to report offensive or threatening content and ... therefore rely on users proactively notifying Facebook of their concerns for any content to be reviewed."

The Committee accepted unreservedly that SMP's had the right and ability to remove any content they saw fit and suspend, shut down or block the account(s) of individuals who it felt had transgressed either its Terms and Conditions (T&C's) or Community Policies. But it was highly critical of SMP's, particularly Facebook, for failing to monitor and report all of the dangerous, harmful and threatening content transmitted by the killers in the months before the murder, although Facebook had provably shut down numerous accounts used by them over a period of years. Publicly, the Committee labelled Facebook a *"safe haven for*

---

[57] Article 74, GDPR.

[58] Article 75, GDPR.

[59] Article 146, GDPR.

[60] Defined at Article 4(7) GDPR.

[61] Defined at Article 4(8) GDPR.

[62] Article 43, European Union Directive 2000/31/EC

[63] Section 1(1)(2) Data Protection Act 2018

[64] Intelligence and Security Committee of Parliament: Report on the intelligence relating to the murder of Fusilier Lee Rigby. Chair: The Rt. Hon. Sir Malcolm Rifkind, MP. Presented to Parliament pursuant to section 3 of the Justice and Security Act 2013 Ordered by the House of Commons to be printed on 25 November 2014.

[65] At 434, Report on the intelligence relating to the murder of Fusilier Lee Rigby.

[66] At 434: responses from Apple, Blackberry, Google Inc, Microsoft, Twitter, Yahoo and Facebook, a/a.

terrorists"[67] and Prime Minister Cameron asserted that global internet firms had a *"moral duty to act"* further criticising that their *"distorted libertarian ideology"* made them *"wholly detached from responsibility to governments and to the peoples that we democratically represent".*[68]

The sheer gravitas and tone of the report, the horrific, tragic nature of its subject and the huge adverse publicity it inflicted on SMP's cannot fail to have effect. SMP's stated they rely on users' reports about harmful or abusive content and the Government overtly stated that they owe both a duty of care to them and a *"moral duty"* to society as a whole. This must increase the sensitivity of SMP's to such reports by their users. The obvious course of action by SMP's is to "play it safe" and accommodate the wishes of the complainant; or by blocking or shutting down accounts at their discretion[69], quickly avoid potential "trouble".

Parliament's Response

Repealing the Data Retention Investigatory Powers Act (2014), Parliament effected the Investigatory Powers Act 2016 to create and identify new powers to intercept and investigate the contents of electronic communications following the *"Rigby Report".*

Despite Lord Rifkind's clear condemnation of "Social Media" as a *"safe haven for terrorists"* and his differentiation of SMP's from other Telecommunication Companies, the phrase "social media" was neither defined nor used in the 2016 Act. Instead, it maintained the term *"Telecommunications Service"*, replicating its definition from the 2014 Act[70] which itself took its definition from the Regulatory Powers Act 2000,[71] effected four years before Facebook even existed.

Opportunities to Clarify

But the Electronic Communications Act (ECA), also of 2000 was specific, no doubt having *Entores*, even *Brinkibon*[72] close at heart: It clarified legality in electronic communications, stipulating that *"evidence sent and received using an Electronic Registered Delivery Service*[73] *shall be admissible in evidence".*[74] The inference is that other forms of evidence sent electronically are not. EU Regulation No.910/2014,[75] effective from 1 July 2016 and which is unchanged by GDPR, is clear that to be legally valid, documents transmitted electronically must carry an "advanced electronic signature" and be communicated by an ERDS, with strict rules regarding electronically-verified sender and recipient authenticity and guaranteeing the integrity of the document itself.[76] The ERDS must be provided by a "Trust Service Provider" (TSP). The only electronic telecommunications provider qualified as a TSP in the UK is British Telecommunications PLC. No SMP's are listed.[77]

---

[67] At 19. Report on the intelligence relating to the murder of Fusilier Lee Rigby.

[68] The Telegraph, *Facebook 'could have prevented Lee Rigby Murder'*. 26 November 2014.

[69] Facebook Terms and Policies: "Availability and termination of our services." Twitter: *"The Twitter Rules"* accessed 29/07/2018.

[70] S.5, Data Retention and Investigatory Powers Act 2014.

[71] S.2, Regulatory Powers Act 2000.

[72] Brinkibon Ltd v Stahag Stahl GmbH [1983] 2 AC 34.

[73] "ERDS".

[74] S.7(1) Electronic Communications Act 2000: Electronic registered delivery service and related certificates.

[75] EU Regulation No. 910/2014 Electronic identification and Trust Services (eIDAS).

[76] S.7(2) Electronic Communications Act 2000.

[77] EU Trusted Lists Browser, updated 28 May 2018, maintained pursuant to Art 22 eIDAS https://webgate.ec.europa.eu/tl-browser/#/tl/UK; Accessed 29/07/2018.

A legal notice in Civil Procedure is clearly "evidence" and "intended to have legal effect" as confirmed in the ECA itself:[78]   Date of delivery or transmission affects proceedings; proof of parties, locations, receipt and contents of a document are fundamental to a case. Yet the ECA has been overlooked where CPR involve Social Media. Again, the issues of legality of an Electronic Communication were addressed once, but long before the age of Social Media and, it seems, not since.

Validity of service remains current and relevant: *Tseitline v Mikhelson (2015)*[79] centred, almost comically, around legal service in person, examining closely the exact moment when notice was deemed to be effectively served. SMP's each assert differently how "delivery" has taken place, but none complies with ECA or qualifying EU directives. A "bold tick" beside a Facebook Messenger transmission is to the ECA no more than the briefest pinch of an envelope in *Tseitline*. Once again, the courts ignored the peculiarities of "alternative methods of service". With the UK's legal landscape changing so rapidly by then, it may have been a very convenient oversight.

Money: Legal Aid, Sentencing and Punishment of Offenders Act 2012

The effect of LASPO[80] has been to restrict Legal Aid funding, particularly in the Civil and Family Courts. Consequently, by 2016, Civil and Family Courts had seen a 22% rise in LiP's in Children's Act 1989 cases and a 30% rise in Family Court cases.[81] In the first quarter of 2015, 76% of private family law cases had at least one unrepresented party.[82] It is not only the critics lamenting the issues: Even before LASPO, in 2011, the MOJ reported that, for LiP's;

"most evidence... indicated that case outcomes were adversely affected by lack of representation".[83]

By definition, being a LiP is a lonely position, made more emotive when combined with the contentious issues of Child Arrangements and Family Court. Without professional guidance, people often resort to familiar instincts and processes. With 42.3 million UK adults using Facebook, let alone any other Social Media by January 2018,[84] estimated at over 75% of the adult population[85] it is inevitable that both its familiarity and simplicity will appeal when they find themselves in the strange and complex environment of Civil Procedure. The quick, simple and cost-free service identified by *Blaney* will doubtlessly be increasingly appealing and adopted through necessity.

It is a natural human reflex when feeling vulnerable to reach out to family, friends and even wider society. Legal documents, where transmitted electronically can be "shared" instantly with social media "friends", or the public. Often family members, including children, are such friends (Facebook permits account holders from 13 years old). Without the calm direction of legal professionals, it is entirely predictable that Social Media, so often a platform for personal disputes, will become a public "billboard" for contentious legal spats.

Allegations of abuse by one or both parties are commonplace in Family Courts. Of the 255,330 cases started in the Family Courts in 2017, 9.5% involved applications for a

---

[78] S.15(2)(a)(iii) Electronic Communications Act 2000.

[79] Tseitline v Mikhelson [2015] EWHC 3065.

[80] Legal Aid, Sentencing and Punishment of Offenders Act 2012.

[81] *"Litigants in Person – the rise of the self-represented litigant in Civil and Family cases"* Number 07113, 14 January 2016, House of Commons Library.

[82] Hansard HC Debates col 486WH, 19 January 2016: *Justice in freefall – Lucy Logan Green and James Sandbach*, www.lag.org Dec 2016 – Jan 2017.

[83] Ministry of Justice, Research Summary 2/11. Kim Williams, June 2011, ISBN 978 1 84099 468.

[84] www.statista.com/statistics/507417/number-of-facebook-users-in-the-united-kingdom-uk-by-age-and-gender/. Accessed 29/07/2018.

[85] Office for National Statistics: Overview of the UK Population, July 2017.

Domestic Violence Remedy Order,[86] a 5% increase over the previous year and 8% increase in the number of orders made. Of course, the courts and public bodies have a duty to act on and investigate such applications and related allegations under the Children's Act, but despite these statistics, there remains public criticism for the Court's approach to domestic violence allegations[87] as well as concern for the fairness of such allegations on those with parental responsibility.[88]

By viewing a "shared" legal document, a child could be party to "evidence" alleging anything from infidelity to criminality by a parent, further upsetting their psychological wellbeing at a particularly stressful time. Outside of the Law, the adverse effects of Social Media on Mental Health, particularly among young people, are widely reported.[89]

Careless or malicious publication may also constitute a breach of an individual's Human Rights[90] regarding the Right to Respect for Private and Family Life. Conversely, SMP's, "playing it safe" and shutting down an account or assisting in the exclusion of a person's communications following a complaint, may be restricting legal access to a parent or child. Not only supporting a Human Rights breach, they may find themselves in contempt of Court regarding contact and access orders already made. Either way, it seems a far cry from the "fairness" sought by the CPR and its derivatives.

SMP's staff may further find themselves personally liable under S.103(2) of the Children's Act, a small section outlining "offences by bodies corporate", for an offence of omission "attributable to any neglect on the part of any director, manager, secretary or other similar officer of the body corporate." Most professionals would be strongly averse to such liability.

Money Again

While LASPO's budget cuts "beg" from SMP's, Private Investment rules them. On 25 July 2018 Facebook's share value tumbled by 23%, over US$120 Billion, with analysts identifying recent scandals surrounding data regulation breaches and declining rates of global uptake.[91] The GBP£500,000 fine it received for data breaches in conjunction with Cambridge Analytica's alleged effect on "Brexit" bit hard, not so much financially, but in the breach of trust it represented: adding uncomfortable credibility to allegations about influencing US elections. Unhappy investors still wield power: their further scrutiny is inevitable. Not least, they will demand avoidance of further adverse publicity.

Disconnected Logic?

When relationships break down, whether personal or commercial, "blocking" or "unfriending" the other party on social media is commonplace. When individuals report unwanted communications to SMP's, they may exaggerate their content or adverse personal effect. An allegation of "harassment", or even "stalking"[92] is often sufficient to persuade SMP's to comply with the suspension or termination of an account, again considering they are "better safe than sorry."[93]

---

[86] Family Court Statistics Quarterly, England and Wales, Annual 2017 including October to December 2017, published 29 March 2018.

[87] https://www.lawgazette.co.uk/law/family-courts-not-taking-domestic-abuse-allegations-seriously/5066271.article 30 May 2018.

[88] https://familylawassistance.co.uk/2017/07/06/how-to-counter-allegations-in-court.

[89] www.birmingham.ac.uk/Documents/college-social-sciences/social-policy/hsmc-library/snappy-searches/Social-Media-and-Mental-Health.pdf, accessed 29.07.2018.

[90] European Convention on Human Rights (ECHR), Article 8.

[91] New York Times: "Facebook starts paying a price for scandals" 25 July 2018.

[92] Protection from Harassment Act 1997.

[93] Per the GDPR, or Data Protection Act 2018, as above.

Individuals may be informed of their account's suspension, but it is often impossible to be sure a communication channel has been blocked by another user. Furthermore, because SMP's have geared their services predominantly towards mobile handsets, it is not only the SMP or user that affects transmission: availability of internet access, maintaining account payments, signal quality, battery power and device functionality all govern connectivity to an "app". Individuals may also delete their own account, or insist a transmission was not received when it was.

Returning to 9.1(3) and 9.2(4) of CPR 6A, in respect of S.6.15 CPR, where applications must state reasons to believe receipt to be or have been "likely": given all the variables in Civil and Family litigation, Social Media, internet connectivity and indeed human behaviour, can delivery of service really be deemed "likely"? A court's assertion that a specific Social Media channel is "open" may easily be, quite simply, wrong.

Jurisdiction(s)

While jurisdiction is covered comprehensively in all three of the Courts' Procedure Rules, covering England, Wales, Scotland and Northern Ireland, as well as the EU, it is future jurisdictional changes which may affect substituted service most. While EU legislation will initially be reflected in the UK once "Brexit" finally happens,[94] Social Media's legality in Civil Procedure is affected by so many statutes, with legal complexity, doubt and contradiction pervading its use.

In *Re T (a child)*, the assistance of Facebook in locating a party outside the UK, but within EU jurisdiction, was welcomed. But Brexit's purpose is to separate these jurisdictions. Arguably, therefore, the UK courts could lose what has thus far been identified as the most valuable function of Social Media in Civil Procedure: its ability to travel instantly and effortlessly across borders, directly to specific individuals. Post-Brexit, the CPR will only bind UK citizens, unless an exception accommodating the CPR within the EU is agreed with the European Court of Justice. Scrutiny of its pre-Brexit decisions has been advocated strongly by the President of the Supreme Court, Baroness Hale,[95] but it is likely that, post-Brexit, UK laws will stand alone.

Conclusion

The Civil, Criminal and Family Procedure Rules were created long before "Social Media" became a prevalent social normality. Facebook, launched in 2004, is the widest-used and market-leading Social Media channel both in the UK and globally.

The Law has systematically failed to define or include the term "Social Media" in new legislation. Inclusion of its use in the CPR requires the Courts' imagination, broad interpretation of narrow clauses and convenient ignorance of contradictory statutes.

LASPO has heralded increasing numbers of LiP's, particularly in Family Courts; some will benefit by substituted service via Social Media, but there may be greatly adverse effects on others. The Law has analysed neither side, but nevertheless allows it.

But for how long? A looming Brexit may put paid to how much Social Media can assist the CPR: an integrated Europe has meant increasingly "international" families, not least in the UK. LiP's in this situation may be further removed from access to justice if, as seems likely, Brexit also cuts the CPR off from the EU. Parliament may be forced, finally, to address the issue entirely afresh, but only after isolation from Europe, as well as the rest of the world.

The Courts seek the Social Media Providers' assistance, content to engage them as a means of delivery, while affording them neither clarity nor identity. Yet SMP's and their staff face substantial legal and regulatory restrictions, not only specific to their services,

---

[94] European Union (Withdrawal) Act 2018.

[95] *"UK's new supreme court chief calls for clarity on ECJ after Brexit":* The Guardian 05 Oct 2017.

but also where their use may facilitate crime, Human Rights violations or civil torts; stern warnings were issued about the risks. Furthermore, substituted service represents a non-contractual[96] liability to shareholders for which the Courts provide no consideration;[97] should SMP's demand "adequate consideration",[98] LASPO will inevitably pass costs on to LiP's.

"Social" Media Providers are not "Legal" Media Providers: The Law has never addressed the "legality" of their use, shying away from so doing whenever opportunities have arisen. SMP's intended users are "Social" users who will not want their casual, frivolous or discreet "Social" transmissions made legally binding simply to accommodate the Legal System's impecunity.

To assist the Courts is entirely at the SMP's discretion, and the SMP's may make their own rules too: with the various pressures they face, SMP's may simply amend their Terms and Conditions and Community Policies to explicitly exclude all forms of legal service through their media. With global society so reliant on Social Media, such an exclusion would be to the Law's greater detriment.

The Family Court in Nottingham echoed the issues of *Re T (a child)*: the use of Facebook Messenger certainly assisted the applicant, his children and the court. But was service ever properly "delivered", and how exactly *did* the Court decide that it was "legal"? It is clearly time for the Law to assess its burgeoning reliance on Social Media, before Social Media decides to assess its increasing liabilities to the Law.

---

[96] *Rann v Hughes (1778)* 4 Bro PC 27, 2 ER 18.

[97] Ch 4.3 Koffman & MacDonald's *Law of Contract*, Elizabeth McDonald & Ruth Atkins 2013, Oxford University Press.

[98] White v Bluett (1853) 23 LJ Ex 36.

Bibliography & References

Case Law

Entores v Miles Far East Corp [1955] 2 QB 327

Adams v Lindsell [1818] 1B & Ald. 681

Blaney v Persons Unknown [2009] (unreported)

Norwich Pharmacal Co. & Others v Customs and Excise Commissioners [1974] AC 133

Kensington International Ltd v (1) Republic of Congo & (2) Vitol Services Ltd 4 [2007] EWCA Civ. 1128

Ashworth Hospital Authority v MGN Ltd [2002] UKHL 29

British Steel Corporation v Granada Television Ltd HL [1981] 1 All ER 435

Nikitin v Richards Butler LLP and others [2007] EWHC 173 (QB),

Hughes v Carratu International plc [2006] EWHC 1791 (QB)

Smith v ADVFN Ltd & Ors (No2) Reference [2008] EWHC 1797 (QB);

Totalise PLC v The Motley Fool Ltd & another. [2001] E.M.L.R. 29

Mitsui & Co Ltd v Nexen Petroleum UK Ltd. **[2005] EWHC 625**

The Queen (on the application of Binyan Mohamed) v Secretary of State for Foreign & Commonwealth Affairs (No.2) [2010] EWCA Civ 158

MKM Capital Pty Ltd v Corbo & Poyser ACT Sup Ct, (No SC 608 of 2008).

Citigroup Property Limited v Wekaroon [2008] QDC 174 (Queensland District Court).

AKO Capital LLC & Master Fund Limited v TFS Derivatives & Ors UKHC [17 February 2012]

Axe Market Gardens v Craig Axe CIV: 2008-485-2676 (New Zealand High Court).

Knott Estate v Sutherland, [2009] A.J. No. 1539 (Alta. Q.B.), Canada

Daly v Lynch [2012], Ireland.

CMC Woodworking Machinery (Property) Ltd. v Pieter Odendaal Kitchens (Unreported case no. 6846/2006, 03 August 2012)

Fortunato v Chase Bank USA n.a. 11 Civ.6608 (JFK) 2012

Baidoo v Blood-Dzraku (2015 NY Slip Op 25096), New York, USA

Re A Debtor (No 0274 of 2010), County Court of Tunbridge Wells, UK

The Bussey Law Firm PC, Timothy Raymond Bussey v Jason Page (aka Jay Page) [2015] EWHC 563 (QB)

Re T (a child) [2017] EWFC 19

Brinkibon Ltd v Stahag Stahl GmbH [1983] 2 AC 34

Tseitline v Mikhelson [2015] EWHC 3065

Rann v Hughes (1778) 4 Bro PC 27, 2 ER 18

White v Bluett (1853) 23 LJ Ex 36

Statutes and Directives

The Civil Procedure Rules 1998

The Civil Procedure Act 1997

The Courts Act 2003

The Magistrates Court Act 1980

The Criminal Justice Act 2003

The Criminal Procedure Rules 2015.

Offences Against The Person Act 1861

Protection from Harassment Act 1997

The Serious Crime Act 2015

The Children and Young Persons Act 1933

The Youth Justice and Criminal Evidence Act 1999

The Family Procedure Rules 2010

The Adoption and Children Act 2002

Regulation (EU) 2016/679 of the European Parliament and of the Council of 27 April 2016 on the protection of natural persons with regard to the processing of personal data and on the free movement of such data, and repealing Directive 95/46/EC (General Data Protection Regulation)

European Union Directive 2000/31/EC

The Data Protection Act 2018

Data Retention and Investigatory Powers Act 2014

Regulatory Powers Act 2000

Electronic Communications Act 2000

EU Regulation No. 910/2014: Electronic Identification and Trust Services (eIDAS)

Legal Aid, Sentencing and Punishment of Offenders Act 2012

The European Union (Withdrawal) Act 2018

European Convention on Human Rights (ECHR)

Academic and Law Firm Articles

"Professional Liability Claims: Norwich Pharmacal Proceedings and Human Rights". A presentation to the Professional Negligence Lawyers' Association on 25.06.09 by Jonathan Bellamy, 39 Essex Street, London WC2R 3AT

"Litigation Notes: Service Permissible via Twitter", Herbert Smith Freehills, 30 November 2009

Hansard HC Debates col 486WH, 19 January 2016: *Justice in Freefall* – Lucy Logan Green and James Sandbach, www.lag.org Dec 2016 – Jan 2017

"Court "likes" Notification via Social Media", March 2, 2015, Stephen Leslie, https://blogs.lexisnexis.co.uk/randi/court-likes-notification-via-social-media

www.birmingham.ac.uk/Documents/college-social-sciences/social-policy/hsmc-library/snappy-searches/Social-Media-and-Mental-Health.pdf Accessed 29.07.2018

"What Role Will Social Media Play in the future of Law?" Jacqui Kempton, 19 May 2015, University of Law

"Social Media: Anything goes." Davina Bentley & Helen Mulcahy. https://www.lawjournals.co.uk/the-commercial-litigation-journal/social-media-anything-goes/ Hill Hoffstetter Ltd

Government / Public Body Publications

Seeking Civil Justice: A Survey of People's Needs and Experiences. The National Consumer Council. 1 Oct 1995

"Access to Justice Interim Report by The Right Honourable Justice the Lord Woolf MR, 1995", The National Archive

"Access to Justice Final Report by The Right Honourable the Lord Woolf MR, July 1996", The National Archive

"Social Media: Guidelines on prosecuting cases involving communications sent via social media". The Crown Prosecution Service, Code for Crown Prosecutors. www.cps.gov.uk/legal-guidance/social-media-guidelines-prosecuting-cases-involving-communications-sent-social-media. Accessed 13/08/2018

"Intelligence and Security Committee of Parliament: Report on the intelligence relating to the murder of Fusilier Lee Rigby Chair: The Rt. Hon. Sir Malcolm Rifkind, MP" Presented to Parliament pursuant to section 3 of the Justice and Security Act 2013 Ordered by the House of Commons to be printed on 25 November 2014

EU Trusted Lists Browser, updated 28 May 2018, maintained pursuant to Art 22 eIDAS. https://webgate.ec.europa.eu/tl-browser/#/tl/UK; Accessed 29/07/2018

"Litigants in Person – the rise of the self-represented litigant in Civil and Family cases" Number 07113, 14 January 2016, House of Commons Library

Ministry of Justice, Research Summary 2/11. Kim Williams, June 2011, ISBN 978 1 84099 468

Office for National Statistics: *"Overview of the UK Population, July 2017"*

Family Court Statistics Quarterly, England and Wales, Annual 2017 including October to December 2017, published 29 March 2018

Media Sources

Merriam-Webster (2016). www.merriam-webster.com/dictionary/social%20media

"British lawyer uses Facebook to serve court summons". The Daily Telegraph, 14 March 2011

"Facebook 'could have prevented Lee Rigby Murder". The Telegraph, 26 November 2014

Facebook Terms and Policies: *"Availability and termination of our services."* Accessed 29/07/2018

Twitter: *"The Twitter Rules."* Accessed 29/07/2018

www.statista.com/statistics/507417/number-of-facebook-users-in-the-united-kingdom-uk-by-age-and-gender/. Accessed 29/07/2018

https://www.lawgazette.co.uk/law/family-courts-not-taking-domestic-abuse-allegations-seriously/5066271.article 30 May 2018

https://familylawassistance.co.uk/2017/07/06/how-to-counter-allegations-in-court

EU Withdrawal Bill: A guide to the Brexit repeal legislation http://www.bbc.co.uk/news/uk-politics-39266723 13 November 2017

"UK's new supreme court chief calls for clarity on ECJ after Brexit": The Guardian 05 Oct 2017

"Facebook starts paying a price for scandals". New York Times 25 July 2018.

Text Books

Koffman & MacDonald's Law of Contract, Elizabeth McDonald & Ruth Atkins 2013, Oxford University Press

YOUR KNOWLEDGE HAS VALUE

- We will publish your bachelor's and master's thesis, essays and papers

- Your own eBook and book - sold worldwide in all relevant shops

- Earn money with each sale

Upload your text at www.GRIN.com and publish for free